BIG MAMA's
COUNTRY COOKBOOK

Recipes from the True South

By
G. Brent Darnell

Other books by **G. Brent Darnell**

The People Profit Connection, How Emotional Intelligence Can Maximize People Skills and Maximize Your Profits

Relationship Skills for Tough Guys: 12 Steps to Great Relationships

Stress Management, Time Management, and Life Balance for Tough Guys: Creating Success on Your Terms

Communication and Presentation Skills for Tough Guys

The Tao of Emotional Intelligence: 82 Ways to Improve Your Social Competence

The Primal Safety Coloring Book

Cover design and layout by **Tudor Maier**

This book is dedicated to **Big Mama,** who was, in the words of
Alfred Uhry, a doodle.

Table of Contents

Introduction

I am a Southerner from the Deep South, Mobile, Alabama to be exact. Mobile is a place where people have names like Bubba, Shirley Boy, Booger Red, Cotton, Snort, Bubby and Aunt Vila (pronounced Aint Vila). People live in shotgun houses and "set" on front porches. When we visited my Aunt Carolyn in Whistler, Alabama, there was a place nearby called Jernigan's, a general store of sorts. I remember two of the hand painted signs out front: "Slop Jar Junction" and "Collards and Everything".

I grew up with many southern traditions that I continue to embrace. When I think of special events in my life such as weddings or birthdays, I almost always think of food. When we meet, we eat. From family reunions to funerals, there is always "food enough for a log rollin'" as Mom still says. Beans and greens and biscuits and cornbread, pecan and sweet potato pie, sweet iced tea (is there any other kind?), cream corn, ambrosia and the list goes on and on. We called the middle meal of the day dinner and the evening meal supper.

A large part of this Southern food heritage can be directly attributed to my grandmother, Ruby Winona Rodgers "Big Mama" Sansom. Big Mama was a spry woman from Chunchula, Alabama. When signing our birthday cards, she would write "Big Mother", but she was always Big Mama to us. She came into this world on December 28, 1904. Her rural upbringing was simple and harsh. As a girl, she carried water from a creek far away from the house and picked cotton in the vast cotton fields of southern Alabama. One of her favorite memories was riding to local barn dances with her daddy on their old mule. Her daddy played the fiddle and called the dances while she kept time.

She left that rural life behind her and moved to the thriving metropolis of Mobile, Alabama and went to work for Kahn Manufacturing. It was in Mobile where she met Elbert Sansom, my Big Daddy, and married him. They set up housekeeping in Prichard. When Big Mama was in her thirties, she joined the Prichard Assembly of God Church which didn't believe in makeup or dancing or much of anything frivolous. Only prayin', preachin', singin' and on special occasions, speakin' in tongues. But they did believe in cookin'. When someone passed, everyone started cooking.

Big Mama loved to cook. Nothing fancy, nothing gourmet, just good old southern cooking. Simple, good tasting meals that filled you up. She cooked up a storm every time we came to her house. In 1993, at the age of 89, she blacked out while driving her gigantic Sedan de Ville Cadillac. After that, she experienced a slow decline. She no longer drove. Shortly after that, she fell and broke her hip and had to learn to use a walker. She used one of those walkers with the wheels in the front. When I took her grocery shopping at the Delchamps in Prichard, I could barely keep up with her. She would zip around that store like a house afire, rolling up one aisle and down the other, bringing back various items for the cart.

Big Mama and I had our rituals, even in her later years after she had slowed down. Every time I came into town, I would take

Big Mama, Willie May, Big Mama's niece, and sometimes Aunt Corinne, Big Mama's sister-in-law, out to Morrison's or Sadie's for lunch. We would always get a big ole mess of turnip or collard greens and an extra slice of cornbread to crumble into the pot likker. Due to her slow gait with her walker, these trips took several hours, but they were worth it because of the richness of the experience for Big Mama and me. Her face lit up when we walked through the door because she knew she was about to be treated like royalty, the Princess Di of Prichard, Alabama. They waited on her as if we were in a five-star restaurant, paying attention to every detail. They knew exactly what she wanted to eat and they brought it to her so she didn't have to go through the line. They knew exactly how she wanted her soft ice cream and when to bring it.

I used to visit Big Mama in the nursing home, but for the last few years, she was not very coherent. Now and then, there was a glimmer or recognition, but not often. She didn't speak, but I got the feeling that if she could, she would tell me to go get her a big ole mess of greens with plenty of pot likker and corn bread, or a big glass of ice cold buttermilk. She was put on a feeding tube, and that saddened me because I know how much she loved to eat.

Big Mama was always a bit of a hypochondriac. When you asked how she was feeling, she would mostly reply, "Oh, I'm sick as an old mule" or something similar. But the doctors never could find much wrong with her. The only thing she ever took in the nursing home was Tylenol for "old Arthur", her arthritis. The Rodgerses usually live well into their 90's. As my Dad says, "You have to beat a Rodgers' hearts to death with a stick." Big Mama left this world on August 15, 2003, just short of her 99th birthday. If I could talk to her now, she would probably say, "See, I told you I was sick."

After she went into the nursing home, my Mom asked me if I wanted Big Mama's old recipe box. I was a little overwhelmed at first. As I soon found out, it wasn't just a collection of lists of ingredients, it was Thanksgiving and Christmas and my Uncle George's funeral and birthdays, and well, my family history. I felt like I was a holding a big part of our family in my hands. So now that Big Mama is gone, these scribblings of recipes have taken on a new meaning. This book will be her legacy, her contribution that links our past with our future. Her children will pass this on to their children and their children will pass it along to their children and so on and so on.

I have included all of the recipes from her recipe box. I do not know all of the sources, so I apologize if your recipe was used without explicit written permission. I have also included recipes from other family members because there are so many good ones.

Some of the recipes in this book do not contain exact ingredients. That is part of the art of southern cooking. You use smidgens and handfuls and messes and other measurements that you vary according to your taste. I will attempt to quantify these ingredients as best I can, but I have put the recipes down as told to me by my relatives.

My wife is from Pennsylvania and until Big Mama stopped talking, she referred to her as "that Yankee gal". My wife was a little shocked to learn that I had not only an Uncle Bubba, but an Uncle Bubby as well. She freely admits to me that she prefers to spend the holidays with my family because my family "sure can cook".

Ruby "Big Mama" Sansom

Other contributors and family members

Elbert "Big Daddy" Sansom

Although Big Daddy did not contribute any recipes to this book, he must be included. Big Daddy was a character. There is no doubt about it.

Big Daddy was a barber for most of his 84 years and cut hair until he was 82, giving what he called "ragler" haircuts. When style shops came into vogue, he was asked what the difference was in a regular haircut and a style haircut. He replied, "About six dollars". He had a Barber Shop called Sansom Brothers in downtown Prichard, Alabama, near Mobile. This is where he and his brothers set up shop. It had shoe shine chairs in the back and black and white linoleum tiles on the floor. There was a large, oval mirror in front of every chair on the opposite wall. Since Big Daddy's chair was closest to the street, he painted one-half of his mirror so that the customers wouldn't watch the people walking past while he was working.

Big Daddy told me the following story about something that happened at his Barber Shop a long time ago. One day, he was about to shave a customer. In those days, they used straight razors. Big Daddy put a hot towel on him and went outside to get a Coca-Cola (pronounced coe-coe-ler). In those days, Coca-Colas came in those small six-ounce bottles that were so icy cold they would give you an ice cream headache if you drank them down too fast. When he came back to the shop, the man had taken a straight razor and cut his throat. The blood was squirting across the shop onto the opposite wall. He wrapped the man's neck up with a towel and took him to the hospital. As it turns out, the man lived. Big Daddy said he went to visit him in the hospital and after making sure he was okay, as Big Daddy tells it, charged him twenty-five cents for the shave.

Big Daddy loved to eat, and I believe breakfast was his favorite meal. He would rinse his coffee cup with hot water before pouring his coffee in so that it would be nice and hot. He loved to save that last bite of biscuit and jelly to eat with that last little bite of bacon. He said that was the best combination of tastes in the world and would savor these last bites for several minutes before washing them down with that last drop of coffee.

He would always park under a shade tree if at all possible, even if he had to walk an extra block or two. He was a Cadillac man, but in his later years switched to Buicks and Oldsmobiles. And he kept them in perfect order, clean and tuned and well maintained.

I remember Big Daddy as being a little on the serious side, but you could tell that he loved to have fun, especially as a younger man. He had a long, deep, breathless laugh that my brother and I dubbed the Big Daddy chuckle. When he was young, he and Big Mama used to go "Kodakin'", which meant you would ride around all day with your friends taking pictures. I'm sure that at one point in his life, he sang and danced because he used to tell us about when he used to Buck dance, which is a little like solo clogging. And even in his later years, he used to sing every once in a while. In the mornings, we may hear "Wake up Jacob, kindle up a light, if you want to see your daddy in a polecat fight." And another favorite of the grandkids was "Sweet poppa skeeter, tree top tall. Turned all the women's dampers down." Mom told me she was always afraid to ask what that actually meant.

Big Daddy used to say a list of names that he claims were the names of some neighborhood kids in Highland Home, Alabama. Now mostly, the names were accurate, but I think he may have added a few just to have a little fun with us. It went something like this: J.T., Johnnie B., Cora D., Donna V., Ora Lee, Tommy Lee, Bertha Lee and J.C..

I remember staying with Big Mama and Big Daddy during holidays such as Christmas and Thanksgiving. I remember watching television with them. We would watch the Gospel Jubilee with the Happy Goodmans and sing along with the Florida Boys. We also watched Lawrence Welk, Ed Sullivan, and Gunsmoke. Big Mama and Big Daddy both talked to the television, warning Festus about the bad guy hiding behind that tree. Big Daddy loved to watch "rasslin'" although he said over and over that he knew it was fake. We watched a great deal of television, and once

Big Daddy declared that he always knew when the show was approaching its end. When we asked him how he knew this, he replied, "because they all go to grinnin'." We heard that many times over the years at Big Mama and Big Daddy's house. Big Daddy would announce to the room, "Well, I reckon that show's 'bout over. They've all gone to grinnin'".

Big Mama and Big Daddy

A few Big Daddy sayings:

"He would rather climb a tree and tell a lie than stand on the ground and tell the truth."

"I wouldn't cross the street to see that woman."

"Don't let your alligator mouth overload your hummingbird ass."

On someone who was no good: "He's sorrier than gully dirt."

When he used to say someone was ugly, Mom would say, "Daddy, she can't help that." He would reply, "Yeah, but she could stay at home."

"Oh, he'll be a doin' that about as long as Pat stayed in the army." One time I asked him how long Pat stayed in the army and he said, "Well, he got there as the clock was strikin' one and left before it quit."

"He couldn't look no more like his daddy if he'd been dug out of his butt with a grubbin' hoe."

While visiting us in Atlanta, I asked if he would like to go see Stone Mountain, the largest exposed piece of granite with the largest bas relief carving in the world on its side. He replied, "I seen it."

I said that Big Daddy was a character. And he comes from a line of characters. Papa Sansom, Big Daddy's daddy and my great granddaddy, was the Zoo Manager at the Montgomery Zoo until the age of 89. Now the Montgomery Zoo was not a large zoo, but it did have a bear. In fact, on the following page, there is a picture of Papa Sansom riding that bear.

Papa Sansom was cold natured. One cold morning, he was riding the bus and kept changing seats. As people begin to stare, he finally announced, "I guess y'all are wonderin' why I keep changin' seats. Well, I'm huntin' one some big fat lady's been sittin' in so the seat'll still be warm." He loved to watch women. One day he was asked why he hung around Court Square in downtown Montgomery. He said, "On windy days if you watch the ladies' skirts you can tell which way the wind's blowin'." He said that there were two things he was afraid of : "A woman that won't smile and a dog that won't wag its tail."

Papa Sansom riding a Bear

Nanny and Pa (Esther and Alvis)

Nanny and Pa were my grandparents on Dad's side. To Nanny, kids and grandkids were her life. She had ten kids, and most of them had fairly large families. Nanny knew all the kids', grandkids', and great grandkids' birthdays from memory. Even though Nanny and Pa were not rich people, they used to send all of their many grandkids a birthday card each year with a dollar or two stuck inside. Nanny would start out her cards and letters with "Hello my dears". She loved on us grandkids till we were sore. She would say, "Oh, I could just eat you up", and then proceed to hug and kiss and pinch and squeeze and bite on us until we begged for her to let us go. She was a kind woman who loved to go places. Since she never learned how to drive, she was always ready to ride along wherever you were going. It didn't really matter where.

Pa worked in the iron ore mines near Birmingham, Alabama when he was a young man. It forged him into a hard working man of iron. Working in the mines plus smoking Lucky Strikes for years, ruined his lungs. In his later years, he would constantly fight for breath, but he would rarely stop working. Up until the last year of his life, he kept a fairly large vegetable garden, worked around the house and helped anyone out with just about any kind of work, from painting to carpentry. He could outwork men half his age. As his fight for breath became more difficult, he was hospitalized several times. Twice he was sent home by his doctors to die, but both times, he came back strong. Finally one night, after long weeks of fighting to breathe, he told my Aunt Carolyn that he was just plumb wore out and tired of fighting. That night he died at the age of 84. I always thought that if he could just have a new set of lungs, he would have lived to be 100.

He used to take us on nature walks behind our house, pointing out the various plants and herbs. We would pick the muscadines and blackberries that grew wild. When we would pick enough blackberries, we would have Nanny make us a blackberry cobbler. It tasted so sweet and good it was almost worth the itching from the many chigger bites. When the sap was flowing in the spring, he would make the most wonderful whistles out of hickory branches. He was a generous man who gave away most of what he had to his kids and grandkids. He was always the last to come to the supper table. When we would call him, he would say, "Y'all go ahead. I'll be there directly."

He would magically pull out of his pockets an endless supply of Juicy Fruit gum for all of the grandkids, and whenever anyone would walk through the door to his house, he would shout out, "Nanny, you go put on a pot of coffee and fix these young'ns something to eat." Pa was a gravy man, and he used to make gravy out of just about anything. One day, after a family fish fry, he made, much to everyone's horror, fish gravy, which he said tasted "pretty good". I think we may have hurt his feelings, but no one was brave enough to try Pa's fish gravy that day.

Every dog that met Pa loved him, and he taught all of his dogs how to shake hands, from Rusty, the Heinz 57 mutt, to Tooter, the Mexican Chihuahua. He would say "tell Pa howdy", and they would raise their paw up until Pa took it gently in his hand and gave it a shake.

Aunt Carolyn and Uncle Bubby

I remember when we were really hungry, we would ask Uncle Bubby to say the blessing because he always said the blessing as if he were in a race at the Indy 500. It mostly was just extremely fast mumbling followed by an "a-men". That's a long "a" followed by the word "men". Bubby was always known for his cat head biscuits. I was never given any good reason why they were called cat head biscuits. Mom says it's probably because they are as big as cat heads.

Aunt (pronounced aint) Carolyn is my Dad's sister and one of the sweetest women on the earth. She is devout in her religious beliefs and also a fabulous cook. There are several of Aunt Carolyn's recipes that I lifted from the cookbook from her local church.

Aunt Corinne and Uncle George are my Mom's aunt and uncle.

Uncle George was Big Mama's brother. I have the fondest memories of eating Sunday dinner after church at Aunt Corinne's and Uncle George's. I was named after my Uncle George, and I wear his wedding band, given to me by Aunt Corinne after he died. Uncle George was a fast-talking, sharp-witted character who was quick to laugh. He loved Atlanta Braves baseball and he loved telling jokes. He was also a liar. I mean that in a good way, a tall tale teller if you will. When Dad told him about someone bowling a 275, Uncle George quickly replied, "That's nothin'. I bowled a 350."

Aunt Corinne and Uncle George

Aunt Corinne was also a great cook. Their house was always painfully neat. All of her furniture was covered with plastic. Corinne was a frugal woman, and I don't think she ever threw anything away. She had drawers full of twist ties and rubber bands and cabinets full of plastic margarine and Cool Whip bowls, all well organized. She used to love to read the *National Enquirer* and much to our delight, had a subscription. My brother and I were never able to read beyond the headlines at the checkout stand, and our eyes bugged out at the dozens of back issues piled up in the corner. We spent hours poring over the old issues, fascinated by Elvis sightings, prophesies, UFO abductions and 200 pound babies.

Mom and Dad raised me and my three brothers. And much of the time, Mom took care of us alone because Dad traveled quite a bit. Looking back, Mom says, "If I knew then what I know now, I would have bought a urinal." We were not poor, but we were not rich either. We were probably a notch or two below middle class and a notch or two above trailer trash. Growing up with three brothers, I remember our meals were a bit frenetic because everyone wanted to get their fair share. Both my parents are great cooks. Dad was a cook in the Merchant Marines and Mom comes from a great tradition of Southern cooks.

Many times, when running late for our many games and practices, Mom would fix what she called "doctored up" meals. She would take inexpensive canned or prepared meals like Hamburger Helper or Kraft Spaghetti Dinners and add her own touches: fresh onion, garlic and spices, making boring boxed meals into great tasting feasts. We were always supposed to "eat till it was gone". And after that, if we were still hungry, we were to fix ourselves something else to eat, maybe a sandwich. One time, I told Dad, "I can't make a sandwich. There's nothing in here."

Dad and Mom (Bob and Betty)

After looking around at the lack of provisions, he said, "Make yourself an onion sandwich, son". Now an onion sandwich is sliced onions with mayonnaise on white bread. It became a family joke whenever the food supply was low---onion sandwiches for everyone! But you know, even now, a sweet Vidalia onion makes a pretty good sandwich.

I appreciate Mom and Dad and the legacy of Southern cooking they leave me. And when I cook biscuits or cornbread or a big mess of greens, my wife appreciates it as well.

Ben is my younger brother, the baby of the family. He has developed quite a reputation as a gourmet barbecue chef (pork is his specialty) and the maker of the most exquisite seafood gumbo on the face of the earth. In fact, he opened his own barbecue place called Patio Daddy O's Barbecue in East Point, Georgia. Patio Daddy O's is no longer serving, but they had melt in your mouth ribs and chopped pork.

He is a little on the wild side and somewhat imposing with his crew cut and his large frame. I would say Ben dislikes people who put on airs, people in authority and injustice of any kind. I would also say Ben loves to cook and loves to eat. We both love diners and meat and three's (that's a place where you choose your meat and your three vegetables for a set price). Anything that is open 24 hours and filled with the common folk, the disenfranchised, and the bizarre are okay by us.

Ben
(far right with a rack of ribs)

Lena, my mother-in-law, who just turned 86, is a ball of fire. She is a full blooded Sicilian whose parents came to this country seeking a better life, opening a fruit and vegetable stand in Franklin Pennsylvania, just north of Pittsburgh. She is not a Southerner. She is, in fact, a Yankee. But she is such a wonderful cook, I felt compelled to include a few of her best recipes. In fact, the Sicilians and Southerners both revere food. It is such a vital part of both of our cultures. Lena is a very active 86 year-old; she still drives, and has more energy than any of us. When we all went to Rome,

she was up before all of us, making espresso and preparing breakfast. While we were walking around Rome, I complained about wanting to go back to the apartment and take a nap. She said, "You can sleep when we get back home." She never wanted to stop. To Italians, food is love. The more food,

Lena Robbins

the more love. So when we asked Lena to buy the meat for the seven of us for our Christmas dinner, she bought a 22 pound prime rib roast. Now that's a lot of love!

BREADS, SNACKS, APPETIZERS and DIPS

Uncle Bubby's Cat Head Biscuits

This one is straight from Uncle Bubby's lips.

You take some of that white tulip flour (White Lily) because it's a little lighter. You get self-rising and use one cup for every eight biscuits. You add about a tablespoon of shortening (Bubby uses Crisco) and mix it in with your hand until it's coarse like cornmeal. Then you add a little bit at a time buttermilk if you got it, but sweet milk is okay until it's all nice and thick so that when you turn the bowl over it doesn't come sliding out. Then you get you a cutting board and put some flour on it and dump that mixture onto it. Then you put some more flour on top and around the sides and roll it out about the thickness of your thumb (1/2") and cut it with a biscuit cutter or a glass. Put it on a baking sheet and bake at 450 degrees for 10-12 minutes.

Note 1: These kinds of biscuits used to be made with lard instead of vegetable shortening. If you want an authentic Southern taste and you don't have to worry about cholesterol or clogged arteries, give it a try.

Note 2: I have found that if you don't roll the dough, but take the dough out of the bowl and form them into biscuits, they are even lighter and fluffier. The less you handle the dough, the better the biscuits.

Bob's Hush Puppies (for 1-4 people)

- 1 cup finely chopped onions
- 1 cup water
- 1 teaspoon salt
- 1 teaspoon pepper
- 1 egg
- 1-1/2 cups self rising corn meal
- 1 cup of chopped celery (optional)

Heat 2 to 3 inches of oil to 375 degrees. Mix onion, water, salt, pepper and egg together in a mixing bowl and beat well. Onions can be chopped in the blender for ease of preparation. Stir in cornmeal mix to make a stiff batter. Keep hush puppies 1 to 1-1/2 inches in diameter. Spoon batter into hot oil and fry until brown. Double recipe for 4 to 8 people.

Fried Green Tomatoes

Take some big, green tomatoes and slice them thick. Dip them in some beaten egg and then in corn meal with a little salt and pepper. Fry in the grease of your choice, but I would avoid olive oil. The flavor is just too strong. Use Canola or vegetable oil or if you want to go old style, us lard. Set the temperature between 375 and 400 degrees and fry until golden brown. Drain on paper towels and serve hot. The trick to good fried green tomatoes is make sure the oil is really hot so it doesn't soak into the tomato. Flick some of the batter into the oil. If it is hot enough, the batter will pop and spit. The result should be a crispy outer layer and a soft inner layer.

Betty's Cornbread

For thin, crunchy cornbread, to a large bowl, add 2 cups of self-rising corn meal. Add a smidgen (1 heaping tablespoon) of self-rising flour to hold it together. Add an egg or two. (The more egg, the more cake like. Less egg, more crunchy.) Add water and mix together. Add a pinch of salt. Heat some oil in an iron skillet to 400 degrees in the oven. When the oil gets really hot, pour in the mixture and bake in the oven until golden brown. Toward the end of the baking you may want to broil the top to a golden brown. Serve with fresh butter or mayonnaise.

One variation on this is to take the batter and fry them like pancakes in lots of oil heated to a high temperature. The batter should sizzle when you put it in the skillet. The cornbread will soak up a lot of the oil, so you may have to add some oil between batches. Be sure it is good and hot before adding more batter.

You can use this cornbread to crumble up into the pot likker from your greens. Also, there's nothing like a big, cold glass of buttermilk with cornbread crumbled up in it.

Easy Cinnamon Rolls

3 cans "wop" biscuits. (Wop biscuits are those biscuits in a can that you hit on the side of the counter, making a "wop" sound.)

- Pecans
- 1 cup sugar
- 1 tablespoon cinnamon
- 1-1/2 sticks melted butter

Grease a tube pan with butter, place pecans in bottom. Cut each biscuit into quarters or smaller. Coat each piece with sugar and cinnamon mixed. Place in pan, sprinkle the rest of sugar mix over biscuits. Pour the rest of the melted butter over the top. Bake 45 minutes at 350 degrees.

Hot Rolls by Laura

Put in a mixing bowl:
- 1 cup lukewarm milk
- 1 package dry yeast

Let stand five minutes. Stir.

Add:
2 tablespoons butter
1 tablespoon sugar
1 teaspoon salt

Mix in gradually.
2-1/2 cups all purpose flour

Beat thoroughly five minutes or 2 minutes with an electric mixer on slow speed. Add enough flour to make dough easy to handle. Knead 5 minutes. You can shape it immediately or let rise once, punch down and shape and let rise again. It takes about one hour to 1-1/2 hours to rise. To shape, roll into 1 inch balls, and drop 3 into a muffin pan. Put into greased pans. Brush with melted butter. Bake at 425 degrees for 12 to 20 minutes. Makes 12-15 rolls.

Mini Olive Oil Biscuits

*   2 cups self-rising flour (not cake flour)
*   1 cup milk
*   1 cup extra virgin olive oil

Preheat oven to 400 degrees. In medium bowl, combine flour and a pinch of salt. Make a well in the center and add milk and 7 tablespoons olive oil. Stir until blended. Do not overwork the dough or the biscuits will be tough.

On a lightly floured surface, roll the dough out to 1/3 inch thickness. Cut into 1-1/2 inch rounds with a plain or fluted cookie cutter and place on a baking sheet.

Bake for 10 minutes, until the biscuits just begin to turn golden brown. Using a pastry brush, brush the tops with the remaining 1 tablespoon olive oil. Serve warm. Makes about 20 biscuits.

Orange, Date and Pecan Bread/and Dainty Sandwiches

- 1 orange
- about 1 cup boiling water
- 1 cup sugar
- 2 tablespoons melted oleo or butter
- 1 egg beaten
- 1 cup chopped dates
- 2 cups all purpose flour measured before sifting
- 1 teaspoon baking powder
- 1 teaspoon salt
- 1 teaspoon baking soda
- 2/3 cup chopped pecans or walnuts or both

Wash and squeeze orange and add to the juice enough boiling water to yield one cup. Remove pulp from orange and put peeling through food grinder. Combine with dates, orange liquid, sugar, butter and egg. Sift dry ingredients together three times and add. Mix well. Stir in nuts. Turn into greased loaf pan and bake at 350 degrees (325 for glass pan) about 50 minutes or until bread tests done. Cool in pan. Freezes beautifully. Yield: One loaf.

To make dainty sandwiches, freeze or refrigerate bread and slice thinly. Fill with 8 ounces softened cream cheese blended with honey, lemon juice, 2 teaspoons orange juice, dash of salt and a few drops of almond extract. Add small amount of grated orange rind.

Lena's Cheese Dip

- two 8-ounce packages of cream cheese
- one small grated onion
- two tablespoons of fresh lemon juice
- four tablespoons of grated horseradish

Mix all ingredients together. Add mayonnaise to get dipping consistency. Depending on your taste, add more horseradish or mayonnaise.

3 Ingredient Dip-Easy and Delicious!

- Mix 4 ounces cheddar cheese and 4 ounces mozzarella cheese
- add 8 ounces finely chopped onion
- add 8 ounces mayonnaise
- bake at 400 degrees for 20 minutes. Serve with corn chips.

White Bean and Roasted Garlic Spread

- 1 head garlic (about 12 cloves, separated, but not peeled)
- 2 cans (19 oz. each) white beans rinsed and drained
- 1 cup lemon juice
- 1 tablespoon olive oil
- 2 tablespoons minced fresh parsley
- ground pepper to taste
- 1 cup minced red onion
- 1 cup minced green pepper

1. Place the garlic in a small baking dish. Bake at 400 degrees for 15 minutes (should be soft when tested with the tip of a knife). Don't let garlic brown. Cool slightly, then slip off the skins and trim off the hard ends.

2. Place half the beans plus the lemon juice, oil and garlic

in a food processor. Puree until smooth. Transfer to a medium bowl. Stir in the remaining beans, parsley, black pepper, half the onions and half the peppers. Roughly mash the whole beans with a fork. Garnish with the remaining onions and peppers, and serve as a spread for toast or crackers. You can also stuff celery pieces or pepper wedges, or use it as a dip.

Maple Coated Popcorn

- 1 cup maple syrup
- 9 cups plain air popped popcorn or low fat popcorn
- 1 cup broken walnuts

1. In a deep 2-quart sauce pan over medium heat, heat the maple syrup until it forms into a soft ball when a small amount of it is added to a cup of cold water.

2. Lightly oil a large pan or mixing bowl. Add the popcorn and walnuts. Pour the syrup all over. Gently mix with a large oiled spatula. (And don't touch the mixture. It's very hot!)

3. Let cool, stirring occasionally. Break off the popcorn into clumps to serve.

SOUPS, SAUCES, STEWS and SALADS

Ben's Gumbo

Ingredients:

- 3 lbs shrimp or 5 lbs with heads (preferred)
- 2 large cans chicken broth (49-1/2 oz)
- 3 lbs okra (whole or frozen). Cut off top and bottom of okra."
- clam juice (6 oz) (optional)
- 2 small cans raw oysters and juice
- 25 oz (750 ml) extra virgin olive oil
- 8 chicken leg quarters
- cayenne pepper
- 3 cups flour plus extra to dust chicken before frying
- 3 cans lump white crab meat (13 oz)
- 2 lbs fake crab shredded
- 1 bunch celery (whole stalks)
- 1 bunch green onions chopped
- 2-3 big heaping tablespoons minced garlic

- 5 bay leaves
- 1 tablespoon gumbo file' (ground sassafras leaves)
- 3 cans whole peeled tomatoes (28 oz)
- 1 can tomato paste (6 oz)

Double sauce pan for roux
Large pot with lid for shrimp
Gigantic pot (32 quarts) with lid

Step 1: The roux

Heat olive oil in a large double sauce pan. Cover the chicken legs with flour and sprinkle cayenne pepper liberally over chicken. Brown well. Remove the chicken and set aside. In the same large sauce pan, stir in 3 cups of flour and turn the heat on high. Stir constantly until the mixture turns brown and begins to thicken and turns the color of dark chicken gravy or light beef gravy. Add mixture of 1 bunch chopped green onions and 2-3 heaping tablespoons of minced garlic. Stir and continue to brown mixture. Careful not to burn it! This is your roux. When brown enough, add 1 large can of chicken broth, stir and turn off. The mixture will brown almost to the color of milk chocolate.

Step 2:

Peel 3 lbs shrimp or 5 lbs with heads and boil peels for 30-45 minutes covered. Peel the shrimp and save the water.

Step 3:

In the gigantic pot, start with the water from the shrimp and 1 can of chicken broth. Add bay leaves, 1 lb okra, 1 can tomatoes, 1 can tomato paste, 2 cans of oysters with juice and celery stalks. Add the roux and fried chicken and boil vigorously for 30 minutes making sure nothing sticks to the bottom. A good pot will distribute heat evenly. Reduce to gently rolling boil for 30 minutes and turn off. Remove chicken, oysters and celery. Remove meat from the chicken, discard the celery, oysters and chicken bones and skin. Let cool and skim the grease off the top. Add the other can of chicken broth, 1 can of crabmeat with juice, fake crabmeat and juice, 1 can tomatoes and 1 lb okra. Let simmer one hour. Add 1 lb okra after 30 minutes.

Then add 1 can of tomatoes, 2 cans crabmeat and peeled shrimp. Bring to boil. Let simmer until shrimp and okra are done (20 minutes). Add a tablespoon of file', salt, pepper and hot sauce. If more of a seafood taste is desired, add clam juice to taste. File' can be added to each bowl of gumbo as well for additional flavor. Let cool. Refrigerate overnight. It tomatoes are too large, remove and half them.

Heat and serve the next day. Serve over white rice with a sprinkling of Gumbo file' on top and add hot sauce to taste. You can also serve it with saltine crackers and butter.

Ben's motto:

"Cook with your heart and not with your head. It's only wrong if it sucks, and if it sucks, throw it away and try again."

Lena's Italian Hot Sausage Spaghetti Sauce

* Olive oil
* 8 to 10 cloves garlic
* 1 small diced onion
* 3 large (29 ounce) cans crushed tomatoes
* 1 quart tomato juice
* 1 small can of tomato paste
* 8 to 10 tablespoons crushed basil
* salt and pepper to taste

- 1/2 teaspoon baking soda
- 1/2 cup good red wine
- 2 pounds Italian sausage browned and drained on paper towels

In olive oil sauté 8 to 10 cloves of diced garlic. Add onion and saute'. Add crushed tomatoes. Add tomato juice, tomato paste, basil, baking soda, red wine, and salt & pepper. Add sausage. Simmer slowly until sauce thickens to good serving consistency. Before serving, add 12 or more large leaves of fresh basil. Lena says she is not good at recipes and she just keeps tasting and adding what she thinks will make the dish better. That is a good lesson. Experiment and come up with your own work of art.

Clean out the Cupboard Vegetable Soup

- 4 tablespoons of oil
- 1 onion diced
- 4 cloves garlic diced
- 2 stalks celery diced
- several cans of tomatoes, tomato paste, and/or tomato juice
- all the old canned vegetables in the cupboard
- all the old vegetables in the frig-carrots, potatoes, broccoli, cauliflower, etc. cut up into large pieces
- fresh or dried herbs-cilantro, parsley, salt and pepper
- dash of hot sauce

Heat the oil in a large pot. Add the onion, garlic and celery. Saute' until soft. Add the tomato stuff and water. Open all the cans and dump in all of the canned and fresh vegetables. Add herbs and spices to taste. Finish filling with water. Bring to a boil and let simmer for 2 hours or so.

Variation: Add Stew meat to the oil first if you want a beef vegetable soup.

Turnip Green Soup-Looks Bad, Tastes Great!

- 1 bag frozen turnip greens with roots
- enough water to cover greens
- 1 can Great Northern beans
- 1 can Navy beans
- 1 package Knox dry vegetable soup mix
- 1 large onion chopped
- 1 package link sausage sliced
- 1 to 2 tablespoons Tabasco sauce
- salt and pepper to taste

Dump all ingredients in a large pot and cook on medium heat for one hour or longer. Serve with corn bread.

Bob's Oyster stew

- 1/2 cup butter
- 1 cup minced celery
- 3 tablespoons minced shallots
- 1 quart half-and-half cream
- 2 (12 ounce) containers fresh shucked oysters, undrained

- salt and ground black pepper to taste
- 1 pinch cayenne pepper, or to taste

Saute celery and shallots in butter. Heat half-and-half on low heat and add butter mixture. When it is hot, add oysters and spices. Serve with oyster crackers and a little hot sauce.

Carolyn's Potato Salad

- 6 or 7 large potatoes in peels

Boil until done. Peel and chop into small hunks. Let potatoes cool a bit before mixing. Boil 8 eggs and peel and chop. Add dill pickles chopped to taste-usually 3 or 4 large ones. Add a small jar of chopped pimentos. Add celery salt or celery seed to taste plus salt and pepper and 5 or 6 large tablespoons of mayonnaise. Mix well, mashing the potatoes a little as you stir.

Ruby Sansom's Good Cranberry Salad

- 1 lb. whole cranberries
- 4 oranges
- #2 can crushed pineapple
- 2-1/2 cups sugar
- 2 cups pecans
- 3 packages of strawberry or raspberry Jello
- 2 cups hot water

Grind cranberries, oranges and pecans. Pour 2 cups hot water into Jello. Add ingredients. Put in refrigerator to congeal after mixing with the rest of the ingredients.

Strawberry Salad

- 2 packages small strawberry Jello
- 2-10 ounce packages of frozen strawberries
- 1 large can of crushed pineapple drained
- 3 mashed bananas
- 1 cup pecans
- 1 pint sour cream

Dissolve Jello into 1 cup of hot water. Add drained pineapple, bananas, strawberries and nuts. Put 1/2 of mixture into pan and let congeal. When it has set, pour sour cream over the congealed salad. Then add the other half of the Jello mixture. Let congeal.

Fruit Salad

- 2-- 20 ounce cans pineapple chunks, packed in water. Drain and save the juice.
- 2 cans mandarin oranges, drained
- 1-- 11 ounce can maraschino cherries, drained
- A small package instant vanilla pudding

Use liquid from pineapple to dissolve pudding. Put fruit in bowl. Pour pudding mixture over fruit, mix to coat fruit. Refrigerate overnight.

Lena's 24 Hour Salad
(Andrea makes this every year for her family)

- 1/4 pound tiny marshmallows
- 1/2 pound nuts

- Can crushed pineapple drained
- Grapes to taste, try 15 or 20
- 1 can of fruit cocktail
- 1/3 cup sugar
- 2 tablespoons vinegar
- 2 eggs
- 1 tablespoon butter
- whipped cream

Mix the marshmallows, nuts, pineapple, grapes, and fruit cocktail together in a large bowl.

Cook sugar, vinegar, eggs, and butter together until thick. Add whipped cream to further thicken. Pour over ingredients. Let set 24 hours.

Brent's Cole Slaw

Finely chop a big bowl of cabbage. You may add some carrots if you wish. Add mayonnaise until well moistened. Add salt, ground ginger and fresh dill to taste. You can buy the pre-chopped cabbage. That makes things much easier.

Quick Cherry Pineapple Congealed Salad

- 1 can cherry pie filling #2
- #2 can crushed pineapple drained
- 1 can Eagle brand condensed milk
- 1 large or two small tubs Cool Whip
- 1 cup chopped pecans

Mix everything but the Cool Whip. Fold Cool Whip in last. Let Cool Whip thaw while mixing the other. Let cool for about two hours before serving.

Channel 5
(I don't know what this name means, but I think it was from a local TV station)

- 1 small lime Jello
- 1-1/2 cups hot water
- 1 tablespoon lemon juice
- 1 soft cream cheese (8 oz.)

Let Jello and lemon juice jell until shaky. Put into Jello cream cheese beat good.

Add:

- 3 tablespoons horseradish
- 1 small can crushed pineapple
- 1 cup pecans

Let jell and serve.

CASSEROLES and SIDE DISHES

Nanny's Fried Sweet Potatoes

Take 4 or 5 sweet potatoes and cut them 1/4" to 3/8" thick. Fry them in butter slowly over a medium heat until brown. Turn regularly. Salt to taste. Serve hot.

Big Mama's Southern Fried Corn (Cream corn)

- 8 to 10 ears white corn (Silver Queen is best)
- 1/2 stick of butter
- 1/2 cup water
- 1 tablespoon cooking oil
- 1 tablespoon flour

Wash and clean corn. Cut corn twice by slicing off the top of the kernel first, then cut close to the cob and scrape it to get the corn milk out of it. Heat cooking oil in fryer. Add corn, flour, butter, water and heat on medium heat for 20 minutes or until tender. Salt and pepper to taste. If you have no fresh corn, use one can of corn and one can of white cream. Quick and easy.

Lemony Apples and Carrots

- 1 pound carrots
- 1/4 cup (1/2 stick) butter or margarine
- 2 medium sized Rome, Beauty or Cortland apples, halved, cored and sliced 1/4 inch thick
- 3 tablespoons of fresh lemon juice
- 1/4 teaspoon salt optional
- 2 tablespoons chopped parsley optional

Cut carrots diagonally with knife or crinkly vegetable cutter in 1/2 inch slices. In medium sized sauce pan, combine carrots with water to cover, bring to boiling, cover. Simmer 10 minutes or just until firm-tender, drain, set aside.

In large skillet, melt butter. Saute' apples just until tender but not falling apart. Add carrots and lemon juice. Toss to coat. Heat to serving temperature. Add salt if using. Place in serving bowl. If desired, sprinkle with parsley. Garnish with lemon slices and parsley sprig.

Big Mama's Chicken and Dumplings

- Whole chicken
- 1 cup plain flour
- 1 teaspoon salt

- 3 tablespoons cooking oil
- 1 egg
- Water

Boil the chicken and bone. Sift 1 cup plain flour in a bowl, add 1 teaspoon salt and 3 tablespoons cooking oil. Beat egg in measuring cup, add cold water to make 1/2 cup liquid. Add to mix, turn out on floured board and knead, roll out very thin and cut dumplings and drop into boiling water with meat. When dumplings are done, it's time to eat.

Aunt Carolyn's Green and White Casserole

- 2 cups chopped broccoli
- 2 cups chopped cauliflower
- 1/2 cup chopped onion
- 1 stick margarine
- 1 can cream of chicken soup
- 2 cups grated cheese

Saute' onion in margarine. Mix all ingredients, except cheese, place in casserole dish. Bake at 350 degrees for 20 minutes. Top with grated cheese.

Green Rice Casserole

- One stick margarine or butter
- 1/2 cup onions
- 1 cup chopped celery
- 20 ounces of frozen, chopped broccoli, uncooked, thawed, juice and all

- 2 cups cooked rice
- 8 ounce jar of Cheez Whiz
- 2 cans of cream of mushroom soup

Heat a stick of margarine or butter. Add onions and celery. Add broccoli. Separately mix together the rice, Cheez Whiz, and soup. Add the butter mixture and put into a casserole dish. Bake for 45 minutes in 400 degree oven.

Swiss Broccoli Casserole

- 2 packages (10 oz. each) frozen broccoli spears cooked and drained
- 3 hard cooked eggs sliced
- 1 can (10-3/4 oz.) condensed cream of celery soup
- 1/2 soup can or 2/3 cup milk
- 1 can (3 oz.) Durkee's real French fried onions
- 1/2 cup (2 oz.) shredded Swiss cheese

Thoroughly combine soup and milk. Arrange broccoli in an 8" X 12" inch baking dish. Layer eggs, 1/2 can French fried onions, soup mixture and cheese over broccoli. Bake at 350 degrees for 25 minutes. Top with remaining onions. Bake 5 minutes longer.

Squash Casserole

- 1-1/2 lb. Squash (I peel mine)
- 2 small onions chopped fine
- 4 small carrots grated
- 1 small jar/can of pimentos
- 1 package of Pepperidge Farm cornbread stuffing

- 1 cup sour cream
- 1 can of cream of chicken soup undiluted

Saute' onions in butter. Cook squash and onion until tender. Drain and mash. Add remainder of ingredients holding back 1/2 of the cornbread stuffing. Line casserole dish with this 1/2 of the stuffing which has been combined with 1 stick of melted butter or oleo. Save a little of this mixture for the topping. Fill casserole with squash mixture and sprinkle with reserved topping. Bake at 350 degrees for 30 minutes. For small family, prepare in two small casseroles and freeze one for later.

Vegetable Casserole by Betty

- 2 cans Veg-All drained
- 1/2 cup finely chopped celery
- 1 medium onion finely chopped
- 1/2 cup mayonnaise
- 1 stick butter or margarine
- grated sharp cheddar cheese (a lot)
- 1 package or more of Waverly or Ritz crackers crushed

Combine Veg-All, celery, onion, mayonnaise, and 1/2 stick of butter into a casserole dish.

Put grated cheese on top. Sprinkle crushed crackers on top of cheese. Melt remaining butter and pour over whole dish. Bake at 350 degrees till brown.

Chicken Casserole by Betty

- 6 chicken breasts or thighs or legs.
- 1 can cream of chicken soup
- 1-1/2 packages of Ritz crackers
- 1 stick margarine
- 2/3 cup broth
- 1 cup sour cream

Boil chicken, bone it, put it in casserole. Mix soup, broth and sour cream. Pour over chicken. Melt butter. Crumble crackers in butter. Spread on top. Cook at 350 degrees until cooked through.

A Big Ole Mess of Greens

Take a variety of greens (turnip, collards, mustard, kale, dandelion, chard, etc.) and rinse twice with cold water. Put them in a big pot. Add two chopped onions and 6 cloves garlic chopped. Add salt to taste. Note: For more tender greens, you may want to add the salt at the end. Bring to a boil and simmer for 4-5 hours. If you want the traditional southern recipe, add a big slab of salt pork or ham for flavor. You serve greens with a little pepper sauce sprinkled on top. And make sure you have plenty of pot likker (the juice from the cooked greens) so you can dip your cornbread in to soak it up. They are much better the second day. For a variation, add a pinch of nutmeg.

Chicken and Rice Casserole by Betty

- 6 uncooked chicken breasts
- 3/4 cup uncooked rice

- 1 can cream of celery soup
- 1 can cream of mushroom soup
- 1 package dry onion soup
- 1-1/4 cup milk
- Grated cheese

Put rice in casserole. Heat soup with milk. Place chicken on rice. Then pour in soups and milk. Sprinkle grated cheese and dry soup mix. Seal and bake at 325 degrees for 1-1/2 hours.

Broccoli casserole

- 2 packages of frozen chopped broccoli
- 2 eggs beaten
- 1/2 cup milk
- 1 can cream of celery soup undiluted
- 1/2 cup sharp cheddar cheese shredded

Cook broccoli until tender in salted water. Drain well. Add other ingredients. Mix together and add cracker crumbs on top of cheese. Cook at 350 degrees for 30 minutes.

Ruby's Tuna Casserole

- 1 can Campbell's cream of mushroom soup
- 2 cups uncooked rice
- 1/3 cup milk
- 1 tablespoon lemon juice
- 2 cans (about 7 oz. each) tuna drained

- 1 package 10 oz. or 20 oz. frozen chopped broccoli cooked and drained
- 1/2 cup shredded cheese

Pour all ingredients into casserole. Bake at 400 degrees for 20 minutes. Sprinkle with cheese and top with 1/2 cup French Fried onions. Bake 10 minutes more or until brown.

Bob's Cornbread Stuffing

If you want, put all the giblets in water and boil for a while.
Chop up two onions and one stalk of celery and sauté in one stick of butter until soft.
Pour in a bowl and add a skillet full of cornbread and any stale bread if you have it.
Add a can of chicken or turkey stock and the giblets and stock if you want.
Add a teaspoon of sage if you want.
3 eggs beaten well-mix in.
Salt and pepper to taste.
Add a pinch of poultry seasoning if you want-not too much!
Add a touch of water if necessary so mixture is very soft.
Put in a pan and bake until brown.
Dig in!

MAIN DISHES, BREAKFAST STUFF, DOCTORED UP DISHES

Ben's Famous Barbecue and Sauce-customized to your taste

Barbecue Pork

"If it ain't pork, it ain't barbecue," Ben says. Start with a Boston Butt or a fresh ham if you're having a big party. Marinate 24 to 48 hours in a Cuban crio sauce if you got it. Add white vinegar, minced garlic, white pepper, cut lemon, limes and oranges with the juice squeezed in. If it's a big cut, poke a few holes so the marinade will penetrate. Remove from marinade. Place on a grille with either wood fired or charcoal with wood mixed in on an extremely hot flame. Blacken the outside, especially if it's got a thick layer of fat. Once it's seared, remove from direct flame, place in grille between 250 to 350 degrees. Don't go under and don't go over on temperature or it will cook too slowly or too fast.

Continue to add wood chips as needed for smoke. Smoke 2 to 15 hours depending on the size of the cut. Remove, cool. Do not chop the meat, pull it. Tear it apart with your hands. If you've done it right, it will tear off the bone. If it's not done, finish it in the oven. When you see it oozing and popping and the bone pulling loose, you know you've done something right. Pull all of the meat. Discard gristle and fat. Include the char (burnt outside pieces as it adds flavor and character) when you serve it. Taste it as you go and include all the stuff that's good. Serve it on white bread with a fine sauce and possibly dill chip pickles and Texas toast.

Barbecue Sauce

I learned how to make barbecue sauce by looking at the ingredients to sauces I enjoyed. You can start with tomato puree', but it's hard to come away from that tomatoey, marinara sauce taste. What you want in a barbecue sauce is balance. Vinegar, hot, tomato, mustard and sweet must all be in balance. I recommend that you find a store bought sauce that you like and work it from there. Heat the sauce on low heat. Kraft brand has a smoky taste. Others may be sweeter. Add onion powder, mustard powder, white vinegar, fresh pepper or hot sauce to taste. You can add coarse black pepper, garlic salt, lemon pepper, Worchestershire Sauce and all the things you like the taste of. Sometimes you can add molasses, Liquid Smoke or whatever it is you like. Add ingredients a little at a time. Wait a little while and taste it. Keep adding stuff till you get it the way you want it to taste. Doctor it up to make it like you like it. Heat it up and cook it down, getting all the tastes to marry. Vinegar is one of the most important ingredients. It'll give it the proper zing and store bought brands tends to be too sweet.

Secret tips-Coarse black pepper adds an interesting visual element. Fresh brewed coffee—up to a cup per gallon adds a good taste. Be careful not to add too much. You need this depth of flavor to compliment the flavor of the pork. You don't want to just taste sauce.

Fried Chicken

Take pieces of chicken and roll it into all purpose flour with salt and pepper added to taste. Fry in hot, hot grease (375 to 400 degrees) until golden brown. If you take a pinch of flour and put it into the grease, it should sputter and fry up hot and brown almost instantly. If the grease is good and hot, the chicken won't be greasy. It should be crispy outside and juicy and tender inside. It may be easier to put your flour into a paper bag and dump the chicken in to coat it evenly.

Bob's Ham

Dad believed in simple recipes. When you have good quality meat, there is no need to drown it in spices or sauces. Take a nice Virginia ham. Put it in a cast iron skillet and cover with foil. Bake at 350 degrees until the outside is well done (around 90 minutes). Slice and serve. For a variation, add some cloves or pineapple to the outside for even more flavor.

Bob's Pot Roast

Find a good, marbled, inexpensive chuck roast. Preheat the oven to 350 degrees. Heat some oil to 400 degrees on the stove top in a cast iron Dutch oven. Add cloves of garlic by slicing into the meat and shoving the cloves in. You can probably use six or eight cloves depending on your taste. Salt and pepper the meat all over and sear the meat in the hot oil on all sides. Place the lid on the Dutch oven and place in the pre-heated oven. After one hour, turn the heat down to 280 degrees. Cook for 1 to 2 more hours depending on the size of the roast. The meat should be tender enough to cut with a fork. For a variation and with a large Dutch oven, you can add potatoes and carrots and onions and cook everything together.

Pa's Fried Streak-o-lean

Instead of bacon, Pa liked fried Streak-O-Lean. For those of you who don't know what that is, it is a heavily salted piece of pork fat with a small streak of meat running through it. It's also called salt pork or fatback. Pa used to soak his Streak-O-Lean in milk, then slice it thin and fry it in bacon grease or oil until golden brown. Serve it just like you serve bacon.

Weenies and Kraut

This was a favorite growing up and so easy to make. Just take some weenies and cut them up into 1/2 inch pieces. To enhance the flavor, fry the wieners in 1/4 stick of butter. Add one can of sauerkraut. Heat and serve.

Doctored up Spaghetti and Meat Sauce

We were not a wealthy family, and so our meals were simple. Mom used to take these inexpensive prepared dinners like spaghetti sauce mix and then add fresh garlic and pepper and onions. It made what would have been a bland prepared meal into something special. Take 1 pound ground hamburger, one package of spaghetti sauce mix. Saute' and add the ingredients you like to the sauce. Pour over boiled and drained spaghetti.

Doctored up Macaroni and Cheese

This was another favorite growing up. Mom would take those Kraft Macaroni and Cheese boxed entrées and "doctor them up". That meant adding some special things like grated cheddar cheese or heavy cream or special spices.

Nettie Kenny's Beef Salami

- 5 pounds ground beef
- 1/2 teaspoon garlic salt
- 1-1/2 tablespoons salt
- 5 teaspoons curing salt (Morton's Tender Quick meat cure)
- 5 teaspoons mustard seed
- 2 teaspoons black pepper
- 1/2 bottle peppercorns (1-3/4 ounce bottle)

Mix well and refrigerate 24 hours. Kneed 5 times during the 24 hours. Roll into three round sausages. Bake in broiler pan in 180 degree oven for 8 hours.

"It's nice to be important, but it's more important to be nice." Nettie Kenny

Chicken Pie

- Large fryer
- 2 cups chicken broth
- 1 can cream of chicken soup
- 4 boiled eggs
- 1 cup self rising flour
- 1 cup of sweet milk (not buttermilk)
- 1 stick of butter or margarine

Boil a large fryer until tender. Remove skin and bones. Line dish with chicken torn to pieces. Mix 2 cups broth and 1 can of cream of chicken soup. Pour over chicken. Slice 4 boiled eggs over soup mixture. Mix one cup self rising flour and one cup sweet milk until all lumps are dissolved. Add one stick melted butter or margarine to flour and milk. Then pour over chicken. Bake one hour at 350 degrees.

Aunt Carolyn's Chicken Pot Pie

- 2 cups chopped chicken
- 1 can mixed vegetables drained
- 1 can cream of chicken soup
- 1 stick margarine melted
- 1 can chicken broth
- 1 cup self-rising flour
- 1 cup buttermilk

Mix chicken, vegetables, soup and broth, salt and pepper to taste. Put into greased casserole or baking pan. Crust: Mix well flour, milk and melted butter. Pour over chicken and vegetable mixture. Be sure your pan is deep enough to give mixture room to bubble. Bake at 350 degrees for 30 minutes until crust is brown.

Chicken or Beef Stroganoff by Betty

- 2 cups or more of cooked egg noodles
- 1 cooked fryer taken from bone or beef roast
- 1 can condensed cream of mushroom soup
- 1 carton sour cream
- 1 bell pepper cut fine
- 2 onions cut fine
- 1 teaspoon paprika

Saute' pepper and onions in butter. Add all ingredients together. Let simmer on top of stove for a few minutes or put in baking dish and cook for about 30 minutes. Cook fryer or beef in foil or Dutch oven at low temperature until tender. Add broth to soup. Pour into noodle mixture.

Chicken in Red Wine

- 3 lb. chicken pieces
- 2 tablespoons butter or margarine
- 1 medium clove garlic minced
- 1 bottle (12 oz.) Regina cooking Burgundy
- 1 bay leaf
- 1/4 teaspoon each thyme and marjoram
- 1 can (8 oz.) white onions drained and rinsed
- 1 can (3 oz.) whole mushrooms drained

In large skillet, brown chicken well in butter, add burgundy and spices. Simmer 45 minutes or until chicken is tender. During last five minutes, add onions and mushrooms. Thicken sauce with two tablespoons flour, 1/4 cup water made into paste. Mix well.

DESSERTS

This category is by far my favorite. It is also the category with the most recipes. Enjoy!

CAKES and COBBLERS

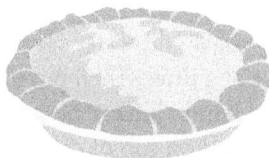

Icing for Decorated Cakes by Kathy

- 1/2 cup Crisco
- 1/2 cup butter or oleo
- 1/8 teaspoon salt
- 1/2 cup water
- 1-1/2 teaspoons vanilla extract
- 1-1/2 teaspoons butter flavoring
- 2 lb. Confectioner's sugar (sifted)

Cream butter and Crisco. Add gradually the sugar and water. Add flavorings. Beat at high speed until light and fluffy. Keep covered and cool.

Lemon Cake

1 box Duncan Hines Butter and three egg cake mix. Instead of water in the mix, I like apricot nectar. Cook as directed.

Lemon filling:

- 1 cup water
- 1 cup sugar
- 2 level tablespoons corn starch or a little less
- 1 egg yolk
- juice and grated rind of one lemon
- pinch of salt

Boil water and add sugar. Moisten corn starch with a little cold water. Add to sugar and water. Then beat yolk of egg. Add yolk to mixture a little at a time. Then put all into mixture. Let cook until done, then add lemon juice, rind and salt. Let cool a little and put between layers and on top of cake. Add pecans-optional.

Easy Fruit Cobbler

- 1 stick butter
- 1 cup sugar
- 1 cup milk
- 1 cup self rising flour
- 1 #2 can apples or peaches or fruit cocktail drained

Melt butter. Pour into bottom of a 9" X 13" pan. Mix sugar, flour and milk. Drain fruit and put into pan until bottom is well covered. Usually 2 small cans will do. Cover with the flour mixture. Bake at 300 degrees until brown. Serve with ice cream. With cans of peach and apple, season with brown sugar and a sprinkle of cinnamon. You may use cans of pie mix fruit or frozen fruit.

Pea Picking Cake by Voncile's friend

- 1 box yellow butter cake mix
- 4 eggs
- 1 small can Mandarin orange and juice
- 1/2 cup cooking oil

Beat all ingredients together until well blended. Pour into 3 greased 9 inch cake pans. Bake at 350 degrees for 25 to 30 minutes. Cool good.

Filling:

- 1 large Cool Whip
- 1 large can crushed pineapple and juice
- 1 small box instant vanilla pudding cooked

Mix pineapple into instant pudding. Fold mixture into Cool Whip. Spread between and on top of the three layers. Keep in refrigerator.

Esther's Mayonnaise Cake

Nanny used to make this cake for us. She liked to use Betty Crocker canned icing.

- 3 cups all purpose flour
- 1-1/2 cups sugar
- 1/3 cup cocoa
- 2-1/4 teaspoons baking soda
- 1-1/2 cup mayonnaise
- 1-1/2 cup water
- 1-1/2 teaspoons vanilla

Sift together dry ingredients. Stir in mayo. Gradually stir in water and vanilla until smooth and well mixed. Pour into two 9 inch layer pans or one 9 x 13 pan. Bake at 350 degrees about 30 minutes or until cake springs back when touched. Frost with chocolate or cream cheese icing. You can put nuts on top if you like.

Candy Orange Slice Cake (from Aunt Carolyn)

Cream 1 cup butter and 2 cups sugar. Add four eggs one at a time. Beat well. Add 1/2 cup buttermilk and 1 teaspoon baking soda. Mix well. Add 3-1/2 cups all purpose flour a cup at a time. Mix well. Add 1 pound candy orange slices chopped and 2 cups chopped nuts. Mix well. Batter will be stiff. Bake at 350 degrees for 2-1/2 hours. Can be baked in round 9 inch pans or tube pan-well greased and floured.

Ruby Sansom's Chocolate Cake

- 1 box Pillsbury Chocolate Pudding and Cake Mix
- 1 cup mayonnaise
- 1 cup water (7 oz.)
- 3 eggs

Mix cake mix and mayonnaise. Add water gradually then one egg at a time. Pour into two 9 inch well greased cake pans or 1 sheet pan. Bake at 350 degrees until done.

Chocolate Pound Cake

- 5 eggs
- 2 teaspoon vanilla
- 3 cups sugar
- 3 cups flour-2 plain and 1 self-rising
- 5 heaping tablespoons cocoa
- 1 cup sweet milk
- 2 sticks butter

Sift together the flour and cocoa (three times). Cream butter and sugar. Add eggs one at a time. Beat one minute after each egg. Add vanilla. Add flour and cocoa mixture and milk alternately. Put in pound cake pan and bake at 350 degrees until done.

Snow Ball Cake by Voncile's Friend

- 2 packages plain gelatin
- 1 number 2 can crushed pineapple
- 3/4 cup sugar
- 1/2 teaspoon salt
- 1 tablespoon lemon juice
- 2 packages dream whip
- 1 large angel food cake store bought or baked

Dissolve gelatin in 4 tablespoons cold water. Add 1 cup boiling water. Add crushed pineapple and lemon juice, salt and sugar. Mix well and chill. When mixture is partly congealed, beat one package of dream whip as directed on box and fold into pineapple mixture. Line a large bowl with Saran Wrap. Break up cake into bite sized pieces and layer with pineapple mixture ending with cake on top. Chill overnight. Then turn out on a plate, remove Saran Wrap and frost with other package of Dream Whip. Sprinkle with coconut or pecans.

Sour Cream Coffee Cake

One box Duncan Hines Butter Recipe Golden Cake Mix

Add:

- 1/2 cup sugar
- 3/4 cup cooking oil
- 4 eggs
- 1/2 pint sour cream (1 cup)
- 1 cup chopped nuts

Pour 1/2 of the batter into greased and floured tube pan.
Mix and sprinkle on top of this batter: 3 tablespoons sugar, 2 tablespoons cinnamon.
Add remaining batter. Bake at 325 degrees for 55 to 60 minutes.

Pound Cake by Elaine

- 3 cups sugar
- 3 cups cake flour (Swan's Down)
- 1 teaspoon baking powder
- 1-1/2 cups Crisco
- 1/2 teaspoon salt
- 5 eggs. Let eggs come to room temperature

Blend or cream Crisco and sugar. Add 1 egg at a time.
Sift flour and 1 teaspoon baking powder and 1/2 teaspoon salt.

Prepare the following:

- 1 cup sweet milk
- 1 teaspoon vanilla extract
- 1 teaspoon lemon extract

Alternate flour mixture with milk mixture until all is blended.
Bake at 350 degrees for 1 hour to 1 hour and 15 minutes.

PIES, PUDDINGS and JELLO DISHES

Oh My Goodness Pie by Aunt Corinne

- 1/2 cup all purpose flour
- 1 cup sugar
- 2 slightly beaten eggs
- 1 stick margarine or butter melted and cooled
- 1 teaspoon vanilla
- 1 package butterscotch morsels
- 1 cup chopped nuts
- 2 pie shells baked

Mix flour and sugar. Add eggs, margarine and vanilla. Add one package butterscotch morsels. Add one cup coarsely chopped pecans or walnuts. Pour into baked pie shells (2 deep dish or three regular 9" pie shells). Bake for 30 minutes at 350 degrees.

Pecan Pie

- 1 cup sugar
- 1 cup white Karo syrup
- 3 eggs
- 1/4 cup butter
- tablespoon flour
- tablespoon vanilla
- 1 cup pecans
- prepared, unbaked pie shell

Mix sugar, butter and flour. Beat in one egg at a time, then add the Karo syrup, vanilla and pecans. Bake at 350 degrees for 30 minutes.

Variations:

You can make a homemade pie shell if you wish.
Add chocolate chips and/or a dash of Jack Daniels for a different taste.

Peach Pie by Veda Harrison

- 5 tablespoons sugar
- 3 tablespoons butter
- 1 egg
- 5 tablespoons flour
- 2 teaspoons vanilla
- Hot peach or other fruit pie filling.

Mix first five ingredients together and drop onto hot peaches or other fruit. Bake brown.

Lena's Perfect Apple Pie

- 3/4cup sugar
- 2 tablespoons flour
- 1 teaspoon cinnamon
- 1/2 teaspoon fresh ground nutmeg
- 1/4 teaspoon salt
- 7 cups thick sliced apples (tart apples, Granny Smith) 2-1/2 pounds
- 2 tablespoons lemon juice

Ready made pie crust or made from scratch-see below

Pie crust:

- 2-1/2 cups flour
- 1 cup Crisco plus 3 tablespoon
- 1 egg
- 1 tablespoon apple cider vinegar
- 1 teaspoon salt
- 1/3 cup cold water

Mix the flour and Crisco together. Mix egg, vinegar, and salt together and beat. Mix the egg mixture into the flour mixture. Put 1/3 cup cold water and roll into a big ball. Let it stand for five minutes or put in refrigerator for later. Take wax paper with some flour sprinkled on top and roll the ball out very thin. You will need a sheet for the bottom crust and a sheet for the top crust.

In a small bowl, mix sugar, flour, cinnamon, nutmeg, and salt. In a large bowl, toss apples with lemon juice. When ready to fill bottom crust, add sugar mixture to sliced apples and toss lightly to combine. Place apples on bottom crust and dot with butter. Carefully place pastry on top of apples. Make several gashes near center for steam vents.

Bake at 425 degrees for 45 to 50 minutes or until apples are tender and crust is golden. For a shining glazed top, brush top crust with one beaten egg and 1 tablespoon water. Note: Always grease the pie plate with Crisco. It makes the bottom of your crust nice and brown.

Lemon Meringue Pie by Aunt Francis

- 5 tablespoons corn starch
- 2 cups water
- 1 cup sugar
- 1/4 teaspoon salt
- 3 egg yolks
- 2 tablespoons butter
- Juice and grated rind of one lemon

Mix corn starch, sugar, salt and 1/2 cup water in top of double boiler. Stir until smooth. Add remainder of water. Cook over boiling water about 10 minutes until thick. Gradually pour hot mixture over beaten egg yolks, then return to double boiler. Cook until thick. Remove from heat and add butter, lemon juice and rind. Pour into baked pie shell. Cover with meringue and bake until golden brown.

Meringue

Beat 3 egg whites until stiff but not dry. Add 6 tablespoons sugar one at a time. Add one teaspoon vanilla.

Old Fashioned Country Chocolate Pie by Aunt Francis

- 1 cup sugar
- 5 tablespoons cocoa
- 5 tablespoons corn starch
- 2 cups milk
- 3 egg yolks
- 1 tablespoon butter

In double boiler, mix sugar, cocoa and corn starch. In a bowl, beat

3 egg yolks and milk. Pour half of this to the dry ingredients, stirring constantly. When stirred well, add remaining liquid to mix. As it thickens, add butter and stir well. Pour into baked pie shell and let it cool. Add meringue similar to the lemon pie-see above.

Deluxe Banana Pudding

- 1-8 ounce cream cheese
- 1 can condensed milk (14 ounce)
- 2 cups milk
- 1 package instant vanilla pudding
- 1 large bowl of Cool Whip

Mix softened cream cheese, condensed milk, regular milk and pudding. After mixing, fold in 1/2 of the large bowl of Cool Whip. Start layering vanilla wafers and bananas, then pour the mix over them. Repeat this layering until dish is full. Basically, 2 or 2-1/2 layers in a 9 x 13 pan or dish. For a variation, try Chessmen cookies instead of vanilla wafers.

Pacific Lime Mold

- 1 package of lime or lemon Jello
- 1 small can crushed pineapple
- 1/2 carton cottage cheese
- 1/2 cup whipped cream
- Pecans

Dissolve Jello in one cup hot water. Add 1 cup cold water or juice from pineapple. Put in refrigerator until partially jelled. Take out and beat good. Then add other ingredients and mix well. Put in refrigerator to finish congealing.

MISCELLANEOUS DESSERTS

Chocolate Delight by Betty

Step 1

- 1/2 cup chopped nuts
- 1 cup plain flour
- 2 tablespoons sugar
- 1 stick margarine

Melt margarine and mix together. Spread in 9" X 13" pan. Bake at 375 degrees for 15 minutes.

Step 2

- 8 oz. Cream cheese
- 1 cup confectioner's sugar
- 1 cup Cool Whip

Blend until smooth. Spread on cooled crust.

Step 3

Mix 2 small boxes chocolate instant pudding with 3 cups milk and beat for 5 minutes. Pour over second layer and let set. Spread on rest of Cool Whip (large) and sprinkle with chopped nuts. You can also sprinkle chocolate chips on top.

Peanut Butter Cookies

- 1 14 oz. Eagle Brand Condensed Milk
- 1 cup peanut butter, creamy or crunchy
- 1 egg
- 2 cups Bisquick
- 1 bag Hershey's kisses
- 1 tablespoon vanilla
- 1/2 cup sugar

Beat milk, peanut butter, egg, vanilla til smooth. Add Bisquick, mix well. Chill 1 hour, shape into 1 inch balls, roll in sugar. Place 2 inches apart on un-greased cookie sheet. Bake at 350 degrees for 6 to 8 minutes, remove, place Hershey's kisses on each cookie.

Depression Ice Cream-from Aunt Carolyn

This "ice cream" was a treat for my father's family during hard times.

- 1 cup milk
- 1 cup sugar
- 1 pound marshmallows
- 1 teaspoon vanilla

Mix milk, sugar and marshmallows will well blended. Cover over medium heat until almost boiling. Remove and cool. Add vanilla. Pour into metal ice tray and freeze. Mmmmm-good!

Snow Ice Cream

Another inexpensive treat during the depression. My Aunt Caroline says they used to sit by the fireplace and eat this.

Scoop clean snow into a pan. Mix one teaspoon vanilla and one tablespoon sugar into snow.

Variation: Add a touch of milk, cream or 1/2 and 1/2 for a creamier texture.

Peanut Brittle

- 1 cup white Karo syrup
- 1 cup sugar
- 1 tablespoon water
- 3 cups raw peanuts
- 1 teaspoon baking soda

Put all ingredients except peanuts on low heat. Cook until melted. Put 3 cups raw peanuts in warm oven until warm. Then put peanuts in Karo syrup mixture. Cook exactly 7 minutes. Add 1 teaspoon baking soda. Mix good. Pour in long pan. Let cool.

Fig Preserves

Big Mama used to have a fig tree in her yard in Toulmanville, and she used to make the most wonderful fig preserves. This is my Mom and Dad's recipe.

- 1 cup sugar
- 2 cups of figs

Boil until sugar is melted and the syrup is thick.
Ladle into canning jars.
Add a sliced lemon.
Put lid on jar and let set.